THEA BOWMAN

A STORY OF TRIUMPH

Mary G. Verrill

ISBN 13: 978-1-63489-477-7
Library of Congress Catalog Number: 2021914214
    1. CT21-9999 Biography. I. Title.
Printed in the United States of America
First Printing: 2021
26 25 24 23 22   5 4 3 2 1

Cover image: Eric Allix Rogers, courtesy of the Ann and Arthur Eiland Art Gallery, Saint Benedict the African Parish, Chicago, IL. Used with permission.

Cover design by Patrick Maloney

Interior design by Kristy S. Gilbert

Wise Ink Creative Publishing
807 Broadway St NE
Suite 46
Minneapolis, MN 55413

To order, visit www.itascabooks.com or call 1-800-901-3480.
Reseller discounts available.

The author has made every effort to ensure information is accurate. Some facts came from interviews, the author's college notebooks, letters to the author from Thea Bowman, FSPA, and published sources used with permission. Some details and conversations are based on the author's memory or as noted. Copyrighted sources are listed in the back of the book.

DEDICATION

With gratitude to Thea Bowman and
all teachers who inspire us to be ourselves

Contents

Preface

Welcome to the life of an extraordinary young person: Bertha (Birdie) Elizabeth Bowman, who later became known as Thea. She triumphed in every goal she set for herself, and then some!

An author cannot separate the life of a person from their times, and it could not be done in these pages, whether Thea was in Mississippi, Wisconsin, Washington, DC, or Tanzania. However, nor could a whole story be told of the places Thea lived in or the history surrounding her. It is the goal of this book to light a fire of curiosity in young readers to want to know more about Thea Bowman and the times she lived in.

Using her life as an example, Thea proved that a young person's vision of themselves, self-determination, and values can help to guide them through life. She worked hard to prepare and share her talents of singing, writing, teaching, and preaching. And then she used them for good: to bring people together in a common humanity so they could meet without hate or fear, and enjoy each other's company. She encouraged people to move out of their comfort zones and become open to understanding and loving people who have different backgrounds from themselves.

Selected quotes are glimpses into Thea's personality, feelings, teaching philosophy, and efforts to heal people's emotional and spiritual suffering. Some quotes reflect her Mississippi roots, attitude of living life to the fullest, and love of people. Lyrics from traditional songs that Thea sang while teaching and preaching welcome readers into her African American and Southern heritage, and the richness and depth of her spirit. Her constant singing and expressions of faith were one and the same thing, in which everyone was welcome to join in.

Readers may notice parallels in Thea's life, and decisions she made, with the vision and speeches of Dr. Martin Luther King Jr. In fact, his life as a role model for all people, young and old, was a recurring theme in her life. I spent three years with Thea as my college professor and mentor, where she inspired me and others to become teachers and to teach in a fun and joyful way. But there was only one Thea Bowman, and this book can only try to describe her dynamic presence, high standards of scholarship, and lived experience.

Mainly, I hope this book inspires young readers, in the words of Thea, "to be their own true selves" and share their talents with the world in the service of others.

—Mary G. Verrill

Acknowledgments

The creative spark for this book came from being a student of Professor Thea Bowman, FSPA, to whom I will always be grateful.

Much gratitude goes to the Franciscan Sisters of Perpetual Adoration (FSPA) and Viterbo University, without whom this book would not exist. Corrections to the first draft were made with Sisters Mary Ann Gschwind and Rochelle Potaracke, FSPA, who took time out of their busy schedules. They provided encouragement throughout the writing and photo selection processes.

Photo selections continued with help from FSPA communications director Jane Comeau, FSPA archives secretary Meg Paulino, and Viterbo University archivist Jason Skoog.

Susan Freese provided an early edit to point out issues large and small; her wise advice was taken as best as possible. Editors Amber Ross and Jill Braithwaite added expert touches and clarity to the manuscript. Alyssa Bluhm of Wise Ink guided development and shepherded the final manuscript through design and production.

THEA BOWMAN

Manuscript reviewers Mary Burns-Klinger, formerly of the Minnesota Humanities Center, and Alberder Gillespie, Black Women Rising, provided valuable insights and suggestions to enrich the story on a short turnaround. Appreciation goes to them for their candid and valuable comments.

—Mary G. Verrill

CHAPTER 1: AN OLD FOLKS' CHILD

Thea Bowman, age 4.
(Courtesy of Franciscan Sisters of Perpetual Adoration.)

I'm an "old folks' child," and I never realized until I was grown up how well they taught me values, how well they taught me survival skills: how to face life, how to face pain, how to face death, how not to be scared, and if you're scared that don't make no difference, just as long as you keep on steppin'.

—*Thea Bowman: In My Own Words*

IN THE MIDDLE of a cold winter night in early 1956, 18-year-old Birdie Bowman sat up in bed. She saw a streak of white moonlight coming through a gap in the thick curtains of the hospital window.

Bright as day—

Is it a train headlight? she thought, blinking.

Has the Holy Spirit or an alien spaceship come to rescue me? she wondered.

All was quiet. The walls, the bedsheets, her hospital gown, the snow falling outside—everything glowed white. She stared at the miracle light, wondering what future was reaching out to her.

Birdie wished she could just drive away. Just drive and drive the long road home to Canton, Mississippi. She was old enough to learn how to drive, but she hadn't. She wanted to see her parents so much, but she couldn't on account of her tuberculosis.

"Birdie" was a nickname for her real name, Bertha. Birdie had missed her high school graduation ceremony back in May because of tuberculosis. And she had sat alone in the River Pines Sanatorium in Stevens Point, Wisconsin, for months.

Shadows of footsteps moved left, then right, under her hospital room door. The light from the hall was dim and yellow, matching the floor.

The night nurses.

Keep going. Do not stop here, she thought.

She looked at the beam of light and a song came to her. She started singing, softly:

> This little light of mine, Lord
> I'm gonna let it shine
> This little light of mine, Lord

Then, louder, she sang:

> I'm gonna let it shine
> Everywhere I go, Lord, I'm gonna let it shine
> Let it shine, let it shine, let it shine!

Birdie started clapping, then froze still. Footstep shadows stopped at her door. It opened.

Tuberculosis was a great fear at the time in the United States. Many people were dying from it, and doctors and nurses feared they would catch it from their patients. The fear meant isolation in hospitals for patients, lots of lung X-rays, and many visits from doctors and nurses, day and night.

Birdie might have wished doctors and nurses would smile more often. They wouldn't come near her because of fear of catching the illness. Instead, a night nurse would reach an arm forward and silently stick a thermometer in Birdie's mouth. After they pulled it out and checked the number, they'd walk away, slamming the door. They were not friendly or caring, and they didn't treat her like a person.

That is what this night nurse did too.

I will never treat people like they are just a temperature number, Birdie might have vowed to herself. *My dad is a doctor and he never treats people like that. He smiles, asks how you are, asks about your family, asks about your problems. That's how it should be.*

While in the sanatorium, Birdie thought about her dad and mom and how far she had come since leaving Canton, Mississippi, on the long train ride North. At age 15, Birdie had gone to Wisconsin to attend school in La Crosse.

Now, a thousand miles away in Canton, her parents, family, and childhood friends worried and prayed for her, sending letters of love and encouragement. She was called an "old folks' child" because her mother was age 35 when Birdie was born in 1937, an age that was considered "old" for a new mother in those days. She knew her parents were worried about her. At least it was warm there, in Canton. Birdie missed being at home, where she was surrounded by her loving, happy family and neighbors who loved to get together to sing, and talk, and eat.

More than one hundred miles away, at her school in La Crosse, Birdie's new friends and teachers worried and prayed for her too, sending cards to cheer her up. Rooms were full of people there. She missed being at school in La Crosse too, surrounded by kind friends and teachers.

She was ready to fly on out of the sanatorium—and she decided to get well, no matter what!

I am going to sing through whatever comes my way, she thought. *I am going to triumph over this sickness.* The bright light was gone. Birdie slept well that night.

Soon afterward, she triumphed by recovering from tuberculosis and returning to school. But Birdie could not know at the time that many years of glorious singing awaited her. She could not know that her name would change to Thea, and that she would become a light for other people by bringing them hope, happiness, and love. She did not know yet that many, many triumphs still awaited her.

CHAPTER 2: SURROUNDED BY MUSIC IN CANTON

Birdie at age 6.
(Courtesy of Franciscan Sisters of Perpetual Adoration.)

My mother wanted me to be sweet and cultured; she wanted a child who was going to be a little lady who would sit right and talk right, but instead she got a little "rowdy"!

—*Thea Bowman: In My Own Words*

"BIRDIE" DID NOT always have that name. She was born on December 29, 1937, in Yazoo City, Mississippi, and named Bertha Elizabeth Bowman.

She was born in the midst of the Great Depression. During that time, throughout the entire United States and especially in African American communities, many people were extremely poor. The hard times started with a stock market crash in 1929 and kept going for another ten years. Jobs were hard to find. A long period of drought called the Dust Bowl killed many crops. People in cities and in the countryside needed help getting food, clothing, and shelter.

In spite of the Great Depression, Birdie always laughed when telling people of the fun times she had as a little child while growing up in Canton. She liked it when adults she knew said, "She is so cute!"

Birdie's early life was filled with the care and love of her family, her mother's Methodist church, and families in the neighborhood. In fact, many people attended several different Black Christian churches and joined in the singing. Distinct lines of theology and church membership were not always strict or rigidly official in Canton and other towns in Mississippi. So Birdie likely observed many types of expressions of faith as a child, including spiritual healing.

The Bowmans had settled in Canton so that her father, Dr. Theon E. Bowman, could serve the Black community there as a doctor. He graduated from Meharry Medical College in Nashville, Tennessee, a historically Black medical school that still exists today. His medical help was really needed because Black doctors in the Canton area were few and far between, and he was the only one in town. At the time, many white doctors refused to treat Black people. The Bowmans were well-respected, middle-class professionals. Seeing her father work long hours, Birdie learned it was hard work to take care of people.

As she would tell it, though, her Canton neighborhood was a fun place to be a kid! From elders and from going to church, Birdie learned African American traditions, history, songs, and prayers. Singing happened all day, everywhere—like breathing air, not separate from daily life. In fact, Canton was well-known for the Canton Spirituals, a group of vocalists that started in 1943 and is still active today. People would stop by their neighbors' houses and singing would begin in the living room for on-the-spot concerts.

Beyond music, the real strength of the Bowmans' neighborhood came from people helping one another on a daily basis. Birdie saw how it takes love for people to come together and take care of one another. Singing could briefly take away the daily burdens and suffering that Black people endured. Alone or together, singing was a regular part of life in homes and juke joints, places where people ate, drank, danced, and listened to live music in the community. Music was a way to socialize, support one another, and celebrate life together.

Singing was also one way of coping with the hurt, unfair laws, and limits of segregation in the State of Mississippi. Birdie witnessed life during segregation when she saw taxis labeled "Whites Only" and similar signs posted around Canton about who could sit where or go into what door of a public place. She once drank from a "Whites Only" drinking fountain, which made her mother really, really mad because Birdie could get in big trouble with the law for drinking from the wrong fountain.

Best of all, Birdie loved learning songs at church, at home, and while visiting neighbors. She loved reading, too, and wanted to share what she learned. She liked to show off! She would run from her house to the neighbors' houses to visit, singing like a bird.

"Here comes that little birdie," said Mother Ricker, stirring a pot in her kitchen.

Birdie feeding chickens.
(Courtesy of Franciscan Sisters of Perpetual Adoration.)

"There's that little birdie, running on home," said Mrs. Ward, looking out her door toward the Bowman house.

So folks started to call her Birdie.

Like elders, family friends, and neighbors, Granddad Edward Bowman was an excellent teacher. Edward's parents, Nathaniel and Katherine Bowman, had been enslaved in Benton, Mississippi. Edward was born in 1874 and sang songs to Birdie from his own childhood:

> When Israel was in Egypt land
> Let my people go!
> Oppressed so hard they could not stand
> Let my people go!
> Go down, Moses,
> Way down in Egypt land
> Tell old Pharaoh
> To let my people go!
>
> "Thus spoke the Lord," bold Moses said
> Let my people go!
> If not, I'll smite your firstborn dead!
> Let my people go!
> Go down, Moses!
> Way down in Egypt Land!
> Tell old Pharaoh
> To let my people go!

Birdie always remembered his words. *I am going to triumph and be free, with a free and joyful heart,* she had decided at a very young age.

CHAPTER 3: BIG STEPS FOR A TEENAGER

Birdie at age 12.
(Courtesy of Franciscan Sisters of Perpetual Adoration.)

My mother was born in Greenville, Mississippi, and her mother was a teacher, and she lived in an area where people were very, very poor but very, very proud. They valued learning, they valued music, and they valued the arts. My father was really dedicated to trying to help people, and I grew up with that example.

—*Thea Bowman: In My Own Words*

LIKE MOST CHILDREN, Birdie was asked, "What would you like to be when you grow up?"

She had many role models to help her decide, but her decision was reached early and under somewhat unusual circumstances.

Birdie's grandmother Lizzie Williams Coleman and mother, Mary Esther Bowman, were both teachers. In fact, Grandmother Coleman was a highly regarded teacher in Greenville. Birdie's mother had gone to Tougaloo College in Jackson, Mississippi.

The same question always came up. Every so often, her grandmother and mother smiled and asked her, "Would you like to be a teacher?"

Birdie had learned about the importance of education from her grandparents, her parents, and the surrounding community. Being so smart and quick to learn, she of course wanted to be a teacher. What could go wrong?

Her path to teaching started one day at age 9. A new school was being built while Birdie was in grades 4 and 5 in public school. The new school was going to be called Holy Child Jesus Mission School.

The Franciscan Sisters of Perpetual Adoration (FSPA) were the nuns invited to teach at the new school. The name of the nuns' organization came from the fact that since August 1,

1878, at least two FSPA nuns were praying 24 hours a day, every day and night, adoring the blessed sacrament and praying for peace and the good of the world.

It took a while to get the new school built. Meanwhile, the FSPA set up clothing centers in Canton, which operated with donated clothes, and they helped build the school. The nuns became friends with people in the town. They tried to help everyone make new friends, too, no matter what part of town they lived in. Birdie saw how the nuns enjoyed doing good things for others in Canton—belonging to the FSPA looked like fun!

Birdie asked her parents if she could become Catholic.

"What?" her surprised parents said.

It would not be the last time Birdie surprised everyone with her self-determination!

They said yes, even though it would be many years before Birdie's parents also became Catholic. To join the Roman Catholic Church, Birdie made her First Communion the day after being baptized. These are the first and second of seven sacraments a person can obtain as a Catholic during their lifetime.

After the new school finally opened and the FSPA started teaching, Birdie sat on her front steps and saw groups of kids walking by her house on their way there. They laughed and joked. They wore uniforms. They smiled and looked happy.

Birdie told her parents, "I want to go to *that* school."

"What?" her surprised parents said again.

"That school" was Holy Child Jesus School. In 1949, Birdie was enrolled, starting in grade 6. With many public schools in African American communities in Mississippi being overcrowded or underfunded, her parents thought this change was an excellent option for their intelligent daughter, even though the school had just opened.

Birdie loved learning and loved school! She wanted to be an FSPA teacher: they were smart and independent, and they loved children.

Birdie learned that the nuns were "Franciscan" because they tried to be like Saint Francis of Assisi. Francis came from a rich family in Spoleto, Italy. He loved to spread joy to others and found happiness by being out in nature. He gave away his money to poor people, which brought a lot of attention to him by the local people. He prayed to God while doing simple tasks. He started a religious group in the year 1210 with only one rule: "To follow the teachings of our Lord Jesus Christ and to walk in his footsteps." The happiness with which he helped others made many people want to be like him. Like the nuns, Birdie was inspired by Francis's example to happily love and respect all people.

While at Holy Child Jesus, Birdie admired how hard her FSPA teachers worked to help poor students get a good education. Their teaching was based on love and caring, like Saint Francis. She decided this would be a good way to live, and so she decided she would like to join the FSPA.

Birdie was learning more songs too, like the spiritual "Joshua Fit the Battle of Jericho," sung by enslaved people in the South in the mid-nineteenth century:

> Joshua fit the battle of Jericho
> Jericho, Jericho
> Joshua fit the battle of Jericho
> And the walls came tumbling down

Hallelujah!

Joshua fit the battle of Jericho
Jericho, Jericho
Joshua fit the battle of Jericho
And the walls came tumbling down

You may talk about the men of Gideon
You may talk about the men of Saul
But there's none like the good old Joshua
At the battle of Jericho

Hallelujah!

At age 15, Birdie came home from school one day and announced: "I am going to join the FSPA and live in service to others. This means I must finish high school in La Crosse, Wisconsin, to prepare to join them, and then go to college. I want to be a teacher." She wanted to leave as soon as possible!

"What?" her surprised and shocked parents said. "No, you are not."

"Yes, I am," Birdie said.

"No, you are not," her parents said.

And so it went, back and forth. A long and tearful debate broke out in the Bowman family.

With the way that paths to higher education existed in 1952, Birdie's parents knew she would have to leave Canton to attend college. Although private and historically Black colleges were available, in the State of Mississippi it was against the law for

Black people to go to a state college. (It would stay that way until James Meredith's admittance to the University of Mississippi in Oxford, 1962.)

Most importantly, if Birdie wanted to join the FSPA, she needed to prepare at Saint Rose High School in La Crosse, Wisconsin, where most FSPA lived. Then, she would proceed from high school into nearby Viterbo College to fully join the FSPA and to become a teacher.

Birdie fought with her parents and friends to let her go. Her parents did not want their dear and only daughter to go one thousand miles away and leave their safe and happy home. They would miss her laughter and conversation. Her friends would miss her too.

"It might be dangerous—no way!" they all said.

But Birdie would not budge. Leaving home as a teenager to go to a strange town far away was very brave, but she was 100 percent sure she would succeed. She would triumph!

That is how it was decided Birdie would go to Wisconsin to finish high school and join the FSPA. Despite the risks and unknowns, her parents knew it was the best choice for their smart child, who loved learning.

CHAPTER 4: FROM STUDENT TO TEACHER

Sister Thea at Saint Rose Convent, La Crosse, WI,
where she was a high school student.
(Courtesy of Franciscan Sisters of Perpetual Adoration.)

I love teaching. I like children. I think they are much more
fun than adults. In a remarkable sort of way, children will
believe you if you tell them your truth. Not that you have a
corner on the truth, but if you tell them your truth, there's
that intuitive grasp that children will believe you. If you
love them, they will let you love them. I'm attracted to the
freshness and beauty of young people. It is so important that
they learn to value themselves.

—*Thea Bowman: In My Own Words*

LATER IN LIFE, while teaching college courses, Birdie did not tell students many details about her first long train ride North to Chicago and then onward to La Crosse. Unlike the happy stories of childhood and her family that she generously shared with friends and students, there was little or no mention of a train ride.

It was the same train route that many other Mississippians had taken to Chicago and other parts of the country during the Great Migration to try and find a decent job and better future than the limits of segregation allowed them. Like many of those journeys, it was bittersweet.

In 1953, the long-awaited day came for 15-year-old Birdie to take the train to La Crosse, Wisconsin, located one thousand miles to the north. Lina Putz, FSPA, a science teacher, was assigned to travel with her. Family and friends said goodbye to Birdie, sad to see her leave.

At the Canton railway station, the famous Milwaukee Road passenger train called the City of New Orleans waited for them to board. The stationmaster told Sister Lina, a white woman, to get on the train. When he saw Birdie, he directed her to sit in the baggage car. That was where Black people sat, according to the State of Mississippi law at the time.

Sister Lina immediately refused to obey! A firm conversation with the stationmaster followed, in which she might have said something like this: "This child is not going to sit in a baggage car. I am her escort and she is going to sit with me in the passenger car."

Standing between the stationmaster and Birdie, hands on her hips, Sister Lina was very firm about where Birdie was going to sit. As far as it is known, Birdie stood silent, as she had been taught to do in a time of segregation. When confronted by people in power, she had to be very careful to show them utmost respect. It was a survival technique she had learned from her parents:

> "You learn very early on how to wear the mask . . . I
> learned to guard my manner, to guard my speech,
> even to guard my thoughts, my feelings, passions,
> and emotions. . . . because I had to survive."
> (*Thea Bowman: In My Own Words*)

The stationmaster threatened to call the police. Sister Lina said calling the police would not change anything—Birdie was under the protection of the FSPA. This debate about Birdie sitting in a passenger car was happening close to the train's departure time. Finally, the stationmaster allowed Birdie to sit on the train as a passenger with Sister Lina.

The law that the stationmaster tried to follow had a long history. Seating Black people separately was first based on a Louisiana law, the Separate Car Act (1890), which required "separate but equal" seating for railroad passengers. Homer Plessy, a Black man, tried to sit in a train car for white passengers and was arrested when he would not move. When Plessy protested that his rights under the Fourteenth Amendment of the US Constitution had been violated, his case went to the US Supreme Court (*Plessy v. Ferguson*, 1896). The Supreme Court upheld the "separate but equal" law, until it slowly and indirectly changed. Instead of a direct challenge, other cases made "separate but equal" laws unconstitutional, starting with *Brown v. Board of Education* (1954), so that unfair laws based on that idea can no longer be used.

The train carrying Birdie and Sister Lina rolled away from the station, heading North. Soon the green trees and houses of Canton started to move away, and fields and hills came into view. Farther on, Birdie saw the scenic bluffs of the Mississippi River valley ahead in the distance.

On the way, Birdie might have silently sung this song to herself, a well-known spiritual from the 1920s:

> This train is bound for glory, this train
> This train is bound for glory, this train
> This train is bound for glory, this train
> Nobody ride it but the righteous and the holy
>
> This train is a free train, this train
> This train is a free train, this train
> This train is a free train, this train
> Everybody rides in Jesus's name . . .

Birdie rode the train all the way to La Crosse to start grade 11. When she arrived, however, the troubles and tensions of her travels did not completely end. For one thing, it was a total lifestyle change.

From the first day with the FSPA, Birdie followed a strict daily schedule that started before 6:30 in the morning. In addition to demanding high school classes, she had equally difficult religion classes. She tried to fit in with the crowd, stay on schedule, and study hard.

It was also a huge change for Birdie to live in a large, five-story dorm, with almost 200 girls of different backgrounds, especially since she had always slept in her own bedroom back home. In the dorm, there was very little private space. Surrounded by a curtain, each girl had her own bed, dresser, chair, and washbasin. All students ate their meals together too. There was no talking allowed among students at the meal table except for one girl assigned to read a book to them while they ate. Given this schedule, it was hard to make new friends, but she was still able to do so.

Generally, teachers and students were respectful of Birdie, introducing her as being "from Mississippi," as if some explanation was needed for her being there or appearing different than most of the other girls, who were mainly white. However, a few teachers and students were not respectful because she was a Black person. Plus, she was from Mississippi and talked with an unfamiliar, Southern accent.

Mainly, what may have hurt Birdie's feelings most was when she was totally ignored by some teachers and students who had no idea what life was like in Canton, no appreciation of Southern culture, and little knowledge of African American history. They had never heard any spirituals from the South, nor did they want to learn about her, her family, or Canton. Time and again, Birdie tried to keep a respectful and understanding heart when people ignored her or were unkind. Despite adjusting to living away from home, difficult studies, culture shock, and being homesick, Birdie stayed positive and did well in school.

Then, just after graduating from high school in January 1955, she got physically sick with tuberculosis, known as TB. She did not feel well and coughed a lot for a few months, slowly getting worse and worse. She was so sick that she missed being at her high school graduation ceremony in May. She needed full-time care for TB, and off to the Stevens Point hospital, River Pines Sanatorium, she was sent, with her mother in the ambulance. (TB was a deadly disease for which a new drug became available in 1949. Some sanitoriums to isolate and cure patients with TB started to close during the 1950s.)

For ten months, Birdie saw doctors and had X-rays to track her progress while in isolation in the hospital. She had books and homework sent to her, and she tried to study for first-year college courses, doing as best she could while still sick.

Finally, after this long, painful, and scary illness, she found out she would not graduate with her friends in her original class because she had lost the whole first year of college.

Some things had not changed, though: Birdie was determined to join the FSPA, graduate from college, and become a teacher exactly as she had planned before she left Canton. At age 18, she would have to keep on steppin' and restart her academic studies for the first year of college.

CHAPTER 5: CLIMBING UP THE TEACHING LADDER

Sister Mary Thea Bowman starts college studies.
(Courtesy of Franciscan Sisters of Perpetual Adoration.)

I found high school teaching to be the most taxing. I enjoyed it, but it was the hardest for me. You see, I was young when I started to teach high school. I was coming back to my hometown in Mississippi; there was a desperation in my teaching. There was an urgency in my teaching. I came home saying, "You've got to learn!"

—*Thea Bowman: In My Own Words*

AFTER ALMOST TEN MONTHS in the hospital, Birdie went back to La Crosse and started as a student at Viterbo College, feeling better and with energy restored. She was more determined than ever to succeed in becoming an FSPA and to do well academically. She was not going to let obstacles or others ruin her future, happiness, or sense of self: if the road had rocks in it, she would keep moving forward.

Birdie did her best to complete FSPA religious training, but it was not easy. Right away, she had to finish the first of three steps as an aspirant, which she had just started when she went into the hospital. College classes continued at the same time too. Like during high school, there were strict daily schedules to keep.

In addition, she had to wear a veil, a floor-length black dress called a "habit," and a collar called a "coif." The coif was supposed to represent the perfection of the woman wearing it. She went from wearing a white veil to a black veil to show her advancement in FSPA preparation at the second step.

Birdie did not give up in the face of these challenges. She had graduated from high school in January 1955, and despite her one-year delay in entering college, she formally entered the FSPA on August 12, 1958, back on track to become a nun and teacher.

On that happy day of celebration and ceremony, she made the FSPA's first vows of poverty, chastity, and obedience. Her name changed to Sister Mary Thea, or Sister Thea for short. The new name signaled her entrance into the FSPA. She chose it to honor her mother (Mary) and father (Theon). The new name represented her new status of being one step closer to becoming a full member of the FSPA.

At age 21, next on the path to becoming a teacher, Sister Thea's first teaching assignment was with grades 5 and 6 at a nearby parish school in La Crosse in the fall of 1959. There was a huge demand for teachers because there were so many school-aged children, as part of the Baby Boom generation.

Oddly, some parents in the parish were angry about her assignment. The group of parents were mostly white and did not like that Sister Thea was Black and looked different from them. They told the school principal, "We will pull our children out of the school if you send us a Black teacher."

The school principal, a member of the FSPA, held firm and replied to them with a brief message: "Sister Thea will be the teacher."

As it turned out, Sister Thea triumphed in teaching at the parish school from 1959 to 1961, overcoming anyone's objections to her assignment and becoming very popular. She triumphed over the school parents' prejudice against Black people by using professionalism and her warm personality. The students loved her! Why? She openly passed along her joy and faith by teaching spirituals to the students, and the students really liked singing and performing the spirituals too! This made the parents proud and happy about their children's performances.

Also fun for her first students was exchanging letters and pictures with students at Holy Child Jesus School in Canton,

Mississippi, the same grade school that Sister Thea had attended. They liked getting to know students from far away and learning about their lives, food, pets, families, and hot or cold weather. It was fun for the students in Canton too. Sister Thea's cross-cultural outreach, to bring people together to understand and know one another (even if only through the mail for the children), had begun!

In her second teaching assignment, Sister Thea returned to Canton to teach high school from 1961 to 1968 at Holy Child Jesus. She was very happy to be home in Mississippi. She lived in the FSPA convent, where the nuns lived, in Canton during the school year and took required college classes in the summer at Viterbo College. She appreciated being near family and delicious Southern cooking.

During this same teaching assignment, Sister Thea was still a postulant—that is, in the final phase of joining the FSPA. After more religious study and finishing the summer college courses, she made her final, perpetual FSPA vows in 1963. She brought her deep faith in God, belief in the values of Saint Francis, and talent of singing into the Franciscan Sisters of Perpetual Adoration. She could now wear the full, formal habit of the FSPA to show she had made a lifelong promise to being a member and to live according to the principles of poverty, chastity, and obedience.

In that same period of teaching, the summer of 1965 became known as "Freedom Summer." Sister Thea was 27 years old, aiming for college graduation, teaching in Canton, and thoroughly enjoying it. That same year, she directed the Holy Child Singers, a large choir of high school boys and girls, and she made an album

Sister Thea teaching at Holy Child Jesus School, 1964.
(Courtesy of Franciscan Sisters of Perpetual Adoration.)

of songs with them "dedicated to the promotion of brotherhood and universal peace." In addition to spirituals like "Steal Away," "Deep River," and "Climbin' Up the Mountain," she recorded some of her own poetry on the album between songs:

> Listen!
> Hear us!
> While raucous voices cry of hate and strife and vengeance
> We sing!
> We sing of love and laughter
> Of worship, wisdom, justice, and true peace.
> Our voices are young
> And we sing as only the young can sing

Because we are free as only the young can be free.
Though our forefathers bent
To bear the heat of the sun, the stroke of the lash,
The chain of the slave,
We are free!
No man can enslave us.
We are too strong, too unafraid.
And America needs our strength
And America needs our voices.
Hear us!

Like many locals in Mississippi and people from all around the United States and the world in the 1960s, Sister Thea wanted to support the civil rights movement for Black people. All the world was watching the movement for human rights, civil rights, and voting rights in Mississippi that had started decades earlier. The movement was on national TV news each night and shown every day in newspapers across the United States.

At about this same time in Mississippi, Freedom Schools were established in rural areas at community centers and other places to expand children's education, including in African American history. Many students had to work in the fields rather than attend school. The rural schools were not well supported by state funding, and many had a teacher shortage, so there was a real need to improve children's education in rural areas of the state. Students in Freedom Schools were often taught using a question-answer dialogue approach, where a student would stand up to answer a teacher's question. Later, educators and researchers like

The Holmes County Community Center in Mileston, MS, 1965, with a teacher in the back of the room and a student standing to answer a question.

(Copyright Sue [Lorenzi] Sojourner. Used with permission.)

Aaron Schutz would study teaching methods used in Freedom Schools to see how excellent teaching was done without fancy classroom materials ("Misunderstanding Mississippi, 1964").

Sister Thea contributed to the movement by providing education to young people in Canton. She would later use a stand-to-answer teaching method sometimes in her college courses because it is an effective teaching method that allows a student's voice to be strongly heard.

One of the centers of the civil rights movement was Jackson, Mississippi, located close to Canton. Even with so much change and activity going on, Sister Thea was asked by the FSPA to decide the next step in her future. They wanted her to prepare to teach college. This meant she would have to leave Canton and go to graduate school. It was a wonderful opportunity, but it would be hard to leave her parents, students, school, and hometown, all of whom she truly loved—again—and abandon them in the midst of daily turmoil and chaos in the area.

After giving it some thought, Thea Bowman, FSPA, agreed to go to Catholic University of America in Washington, DC, for graduate studies in the summer of 1966. On campus, she drew

Sister Thea with friend Charlene Smith, FSPA.
(Courtesy of Franciscan Sisters of Perpetual Adoration.)

people together and made lifelong friends such as Sister Rochelle Potaracke and Sister Mary Ann Gschwind. Together, her group of friends became known as "Thea's community."

At about this time, the Roman Catholic Church eased up its requirements for veils, coifs, and long dresses for religious women. Although still expected to be dressed in full habit for teaching and formal occasions until 1962, nuns could now choose whether to wear a veil or coif, providing relief from tight collars, especially on hot days.

Continuing her studies in higher education, Sister Thea graduated in 1969 with a Master of Arts degree in English. She graduated again in 1972 with a Doctor of Philosophy (PhD) degree in English and linguistics. The PhD she earned is the highest degree a person can obtain.

Sister Thea had shown her scholarly talents through hard work and a belief in her own abilities—far beyond where young Birdie had ever imagined. She had done it by sacrificing time spent in her favorite hometown near her parents and students, during a time when her presence there was greatly needed.

As she left Washington, DC, this return to La Crosse was different. She was no longer a graduate student, but was now a professor. She had met her goals of becoming a teacher, member of the FSPA, and a college graduate—at the highest level!

A PhD was a huge triumph over the limits of education that once would have been imposed on her as a Black woman in the State of Mississippi. More triumphs, and more sacrifice, lay ahead for her.

CHAPTER 6: THE SINGING PROFESSOR

Sister Thea hosted a public convocation about spirituals
when she arrived at Viterbo College to teach.
(Imprints yearbook, 1971.)

One of the things I learned about students in college is
that so many come there programmed to find out what the
teacher wants and what the teacher wants them to think
and what the teacher wants them to say. I say you don't have
to do that. You don't have to be afraid. Think for yourself.
Your opinion is as good as mine. So long as you support
your opinion by evidence, it is as valid as mine. That was my
approach. You've got it, then use it.

—*Thea Bowman: In My Own Words*

IN 1972, AFTER her final graduation and leaving Washington, DC, Sister Thea was back at Viterbo College, but this time as a college professor in the English Department. Unlike when she first came to La Crosse for high school, she knew the mainly white, Midwestern culture was not like Mississippi, or even like Washington, DC. This time, she had more confidence in wanting to share the joy she felt in expressing what she knew: African American traditions, African American literature, and songs in daily prayer and praise to God. And so she did—everywhere on campus.

Thea wished to continue sharing the daily joy and faith of Saint Francis and expressing it in song. Like him, she wanted to create love and understanding between people, no matter their backgrounds or social status. In addition to academic reading, writing, and music, she tried to show others how to bring people together—in their common humanity—in the classroom and across cultures. One way to do that, she advised, was to "just be yourself."

In fact, in the first minute of the first day of a new academic year and Fall semester, college students in Sister Thea's literature class were told "Knothe seuton." She silently wrote it on the board, then asked if anyone knew what it meant.

The students looked at each other blankly. There was a long silence.

Then she wrote "Know thyself" and said, "That is all you will ever need to know."

In moments like this, students in Sister Thea's college courses became aware that there was more than learning about books and authors going on. There were cultural considerations to ponder and African American history to review, issues of faith and identity, problems of equity, and historical trauma to address. Students were equally held in awe by her knowledge of literature and Middle English as by her life experiences as a child and teen in Mississippi.

Most of her students were not from nor had traveled to the South, much less heard the spirituals she sang in class. None of the students expected a tall and authoritative PhD lecturer to sing in a classroom that was supposed to be studying classic English literature. Like the younger students in her first teaching assignment, college students were exposed to something new, a new way of learning and a new way of expressing emotions, by listening to Sister Thea sing songs of her heritage, by joining in, and then by getting discussion going about literature. Soon, she routinely added singing in class to help students thrive in their studies and in their lives.

As an English professor, Sister Thea believed everyone should emotionally feel, not just read, literature. By studying intense authors like William Faulkner, Langston Hughes, Ralph Ellison, Gwendolyn Brooks, and Toni Morrison, students experienced fiction, poetry, and drama "off the page," as if their imaginary narrators and characters were real.

But wait, William Faulkner?

Faulkner was from Mississippi and, because of sharing the same home state, he was one of Sister Thea's favorite authors. Even though he portrayed white supremacy and exposed a romantic view of the South in his characters, Thea studied his fictional works and found them to be of great value. Students and scholars alike wondered and asked, "Why is this Black professor so interested in William Faulkner?"

When responding to this question in front of a large conference of Faulkner scholars, Sister Thea explained:

> Faulkner has helped me understand my state. And it is *my* state. My people, as Faulkner records, helped to build it, clearing wilderness, tilling land, building with brick and wood and mortar, and raising those children. And not just the Black children.
>
> Faulkner has helped me to appreciate my state. Both the glory and the shame of it.
>
> Faulkner also helped me to understand White folks. Their ways of thinking and feeling and responding. And as a Black child, born in Mississippi, and as a Black woman, living in America or anywhere, I need to understand." ("Are You Walkin' with Me?", 1990. Used with permission of University of Mississippi.)

Not only did Sister Thea admire Faulkner as a writer, but she also attended the Faulkner and Yoknapatawpha Conference from summer 1974 onward, hosted by the University of Mississippi in Oxford. The annual conference was and is open to scholars, students, and the public. Attendees gathered to discuss and discover the works of William Faulkner and other Southern authors, on whom Sister Thea was an expert. Before long, she became a popular presenter, inviting the audience to go beyond a surface reading of Faulkner's works into an understanding of African American culture as a knowledge base to feel and understand those works, and to sing some spirituals with her too, to help find that broader and deeper understanding. She concluded that Faulkner "understood a lot" about African American culture and did not just observe and record it ("Are You Walkin' with Me?", 1990).

At the conference and wherever Sister Thea went, audience participation was a vital part of establishing dialogue and depth of understanding between people. For example, sometimes in college classes at Viterbo, Sister Thea would pose a question and then require a student to stand to respond. The reason for standing was somewhat practical, so the students' voices could be heard strongly and clearly, but it also was part of an oral tradition that made the speaker accountable for what they said. She also made students be responsible for their opinions about what they read, and they could be called on at any time to defend their ideas. Students got accustomed to diving back into the book to prove an opinion was based on the text, not just a wild guess.

Incredibly, Sister Thea could also read Latin and interpret Medieval and Renaissance poetry, which she loved to read out loud to students. In her Shakespeare class, many sonnets and almost all the plays—comedy, history, and tragedy—were read during two semesters. Class started at 8:00 a.m., and every student was expected to be on time—even in the worst cold weather of winter.

Occasionally, a homesick student would want to talk with Sister Thea, needing a morale boost or academic assistance. Being homesick was something Sister Thea certainly understood from her high school days! When a student asked for some "personal advice," Sister Thea invited the student to her office above the English Department after class. The student slowly entered the large, wood-paneled office and saw a velvet tapestry of Saint Thomas More hanging on the wall to the right. Another wall was covered in bookcases that were stuffed with books. From behind a big desk, Sister Thea asked the student to sit down on the other side and, seeing the student stare at the tapestry, talked about the genius of More and how he was her hero. She lectured for 20 minutes about how he held firm in his faith despite being surrounded by irrational enemies, trials, the king's power, and death threats—it was a fascinating, true story.

When Sister Thea finally asked what the student wanted to talk about, the silent student could not speak—personal concerns like being homesick seemed petty and small compared to More's belief in humanism, faith in justice, and unwavering devotion to God, even upon threat of death. The meeting ended happily with an increase in the student's motivation to learn as much as possible before heading home for the upcoming break.

In a classroom routine, the wooden desks were turned inward to huddle in a circle with Sister Thea, to read passages out loud and discuss footnotes. She advised students to always read the footnotes if the author was Shakespeare. Sometimes, she directed students to act out scenes from a Shakespearean tragedy as if they

Viterbo University and Holy Child Jesus high school
students get together for lunch in Canton.
(Imprints yearbook, 1977.)

were on stage, including sword fights. She explained the psychology, irrational feelings, and flaws of his characters—Hamlet, Othello, Lady Macbeth—like they were real people. She urged students to apply those characters' errors and lessons to their own lives.

In Black American literature class, Sister Thea shared with students from diverse backgrounds her knowledge of oral traditions and symbols in autobiography, the short story, the novel, poetry, and feminist literary criticism. Students from around the United States and other nations were particularly drawn to this course. She insisted that each student learn "what it is to be Black in this country." She selected and required books by authors such as Malcolm X and Nikki Giovanni to widen students' viewpoints.

To better learn how to live and breathe Southern literature, Sister Thea led students on trips to her hometown, Canton. Students lived in the middle-class homes of Black folks, situated between separate areas of rich white folks and poor Black folks. The housing separation was obvious evidence of a long, deep racial and economic divide, according to one student participant (Interview, March 2020).

Student groups visited Memphis and the Dr. Martin Luther King Jr. Memorial. On one trip, Sister Thea led students straight down the center of Bourbon Street in New Orleans, just for fun. On another trip, the group met one of Sister Thea's most admired authors, Dr. Margaret Walker Alexander. Sister Thea wanted to close divides, to be a bridge between people from the North and South, who would not usually have a chance to know each other.

Back on campus, a student never knew what to expect in Sister Thea's class, except that it would be interesting! She might begin her class with a heartbreaking spiritual like "Motherless Child," and the class would be encouraged to join in:

Sometimes I feel like a motherless child
Sometimes I feel like a motherless child
Sometimes I feel like a motherless child
A long way from home
A long way from home
True believer
A long way from home
A long way from home

Other days, class might start with a hopeful yet painful civil rights song like "We Shall Overcome." After a while, everyone in

Students made Thea laugh in the classroom, and vice versa.
(Imprints yearbook, 1975.)

the room was expected to sing because the song had been sung enough times that everyone should know the words.

Sister Thea once said class would not start until *everyone* sang and wiggled their hips as best they could to the rousing spiritual "Dem Bones." Of course, she found this to be very funny! Actually, she wanted students to discover that serious reading and writing were easier after "loosening up."

As Chair of the English Department, Sister Thea directed the thesis course, which all English majors needed to pass to graduate. A thesis is an essay exploring a new idea about literature that a student must discover, explain, and prove—in public. As a mentor, Sister Thea guided students through the process of writing the essay but never told them what to think. The thesis required a public defense, open to questions from professors, students, and the entire city of La Crosse. To ease the pressure, each student presented their thesis on campus, followed by a big party and food. And of course, with Sister Thea there, the celebration included some singing after dessert.

Without trying, Sister Thea inspired some college students to become teachers. Their desire to teach might have begun with her loud phrase: "I am not teaching this class—*you* are!"

She would assign parts of a novel or play to read, and then ask students to teach it to the class. This teaching method was way ahead of its time for a college professor in the 1970s.

Sister Thea allowed students to bring their own talents to the classroom, like playing an instrument, designing costumes, or acting. That is one reason why students liked having her as a professor. She would often remind them: "It is okay to be good at more than one thing." For example, Music majors were allowed

Sister Thea (fourth from left) with the Hallelujah Singers,
a group she founded.
(Imprints yearbook, 1972.)

to play music from Shakespeare's play *Twelfth Night*, which was researched, borrowed, and transcribed into modern notes from The Folger Shakespeare Library in Washington, DC, instead of writing an essay.

Public venues for singing were also created by Sister Thea, who took advantage of having a large stage available at the Viterbo College Fine Arts Center. The Hallelujah Singers, which she founded, performed there to bring faith and joy to others. She joined the singers to "be one's self" and pass along songs and African American traditions from the South to audiences who may have never heard them before. At other public events, she sang spirituals, inviting the crowd to sing and experience messages of struggle and hope.

Sister Thea also sponsored English Club meetings. Instead of having an agenda, these were potluck and fast-food dinners with sing-alongs of folk, rock, Neil Young, the Beatles, or whatever students wanted to sing. Students brought their own guitars, drums, and other instruments for the music-making, and Sister Thea took on the role of song learner, not leader.

Sister Thea was making the world her classroom, and it was full of music.

CHAPTER 7: FROM TEACHER TO HEALER

Thea returns to Canton.
(Courtesy of Franciscan Sisters of Perpetual Adoration. Photo by Jerome Friar.)

And if we walk on and talk on and work on and pray on and hold on and love on in faith, we shall overcome. Overcome weakness, overcome fatigue, overcome exhaustion, overcome pain and loneliness, overcome frustration, overcome the prejudices and the stereotypes, the anxieties, the grief, the fear, the negative attitudes—all those barriers and boundaries that keep us apart, overcome racism and classism and sexism and materialism, all those "isms" that keep us apart.

—*Thea Bowman: In My Own Words*

THEA HAD GREAT success as a college professor. She was highly respected by students as a demanding yet caring educator and scholar, and she was a well-placed administrator as Chair of the English Department. However, a sense of responsibility and a new mission called her back to Mississippi. She returned to Canton in 1978 to accept a new position with the Catholic Diocese of Jackson.

Specifically, Thea got permission to go home and take care of her parents and to teach, and she was appointed Director of Intercultural Awareness. Now she wanted to be known simply as "Thea," even though she would always be a member of the FSPA.

In addition to her work with the Diocese of Jackson, Thea taught children in Canton again, delighted to be back home.

Then, to further speak out against racial injustice and prejudice, to celebrate African American culture, and to spread messages of hope, faith and joy, Thea began to travel more and to host public revivals. Revivals were common and important in Southern Christian communities. For example, many Baptist Churches would have several revivals a year.

In 1980, Thea also became a founding member of the Institute for Black Catholic Studies at Xavier University in New Orleans. Thea was continuing an ongoing struggle, which she had taken on, to have the Catholic Church, different cultures, and

Thea leads a revival.
(Courtesy of Franciscan Sisters of Perpetual Adoration.
Photo by John Feister.)

society-at-large accept, learn, and celebrate African American traditions and expressions of faith.

Soon, even more invitations from across the United States were coming into the Diocese of Jackson asking for Thea to bring her leadership and guidance in forming a sense of community, increased intercultural awareness, and encouragement for people to work together to solve problems.

Then, in 1984, suddenly and sadly, both her parents died.

That same year, Thea was diagnosed with cancer. The onset of cancer was bad news, but it did not slow her down. Fighting cancer became another way to triumph over obstacles and limits.

Thea's constant travels and hosting of events to bring people together continued as if there was no cancer. She hosted revivals, lectures, workshops, and concerts. She got even more invitations to visit groups and organizations that wanted to hear her messages of hope, love, and caring for self and others.

Thea sings at the Diocese of Jackson, 1988.
(Courtesy of Franciscan Sisters of Perpetual Adoration.)

In summer 1985, Thea visited Nigeria and Tanzania to participate in a workshop on racism. She was part of a group invited by the Maryknoll Sisters, an organization of Catholic religious women. She also spent time with the Sisters of the Sacred Heart on that same trip. In a letter to friends and followers, dated December 26, 1985, she reported "finding more of my rootedness and more of myself . . . [in Africa] I met people who looked and thought and moved like me."

She said she was "renewed" by visiting the "Mother Continent" in a 1987 (undated) personal letter sent to followers and friends. In a special moment, she cheerily told of how some Maasai people mistook her as being Maasai due to her baldness from radiation treatment. It was an honor and "a good feeling," she wrote. In reporting on her travels as much as possible, Thea was trying to teach people that all humans share the same things in common, such as the needs for peace, equality, and comfort within the society in which they live.

On the road and not feeling well, the words of an old gospel song, "Wayfaring Stranger," may have come to mind:

I'm just a poor wayfaring stranger
Traveling through this world below
There is no sickness, no toil, nor danger
In that bright land to which I go

I'm going there to see my Father
And all my loved ones who've gone on
I'm just going over Jordan
I'm just going over home

I know dark clouds will gather 'round me
I know my way is hard and steep
But beauteous fields arise before me
Where God's redeemed, their vigils keep

I'm going there to see my Mother
She said she'd meet me when I come
So, I'm just going over Jordan
I'm just going over home
I'm just going over Jordan
I'm just going over home

One trip was especially exciting. In 1987, Thea, friends, and students were invited to be featured on the popular CBS news show *60 Minutes*. During her interview with host Mike Wallace, with a twinkle in her eye and a wide smile, she asked him, "Can you please say, 'Black is beautiful'?"

After a look of shock at himself being questioned and a brief hesitation, Wallace said clearly, "Black is beautiful," in front of the whole United States television audience. It was a public affirmation that many people had been saying for a long time, and Thea enjoyed retelling that moment in a letter about her travels (Personal letter, Jan. 1, 1988).

During that same year, Thea traveled to twenty-five states and the Virgin Islands to deliver messages of hope, love, and prayer. She invited people to come together to pray, heal, and sing

Thea laughs while on stage.
(Courtesy of Franciscan Sisters of Perpetual Adoration.)

wherever she went. Although suffering from chemotherapy treatments in 1988, Thea encouraged African-based rituals, dance, and music in Catholic services, Sunday Mass, and gatherings, working to expand forms of Catholic faith. This mission of change and inclusion became one of her most profound contributions to the Catholic Church. Since that time, attention to and inclusion of cultural expression has been included in Sunday Mass and other rituals, an expansion of an effort inspired by and supported by Thea.

Whatever difficulty, roadblock, or challenge came into Thea's life, she could turn it into a joyous, positive change and inspire others to do the same.

CHAPTER 8: LIKE A SHOOTING STAR

Thea's image in the Ann and Arthur Eiland Art Gallery, Saint Benedict the African Parish, Chicago, IL.

(Copyright Eric Allix Rogers. Used with permission.)

I can be a bridge over troubled water. I can take you by the hand and take you with me into the Black community. I can walk you into your community, and if I walk with you into your community, I don't walk as a stranger, I walk as your sister.

—*Thea Bowman: In My Own Words*

59

WITHOUT SEEKING FAME, news of Thea's outreach became widely known. She created chances and worked hard to expand the Catholic Church's masses and rituals to include African American music, traditions, and culture. In one project, she worked with a bishop to create a hymnal for Catholics that contained spirituals.

More chances to highlight, include, and preserve African American culture and traditions also occurred:

- Thea talked with Harry Belafonte, a film producer, who visited her in New Orleans in 1988, about a movie based on her life. Actress Whoopi Goldberg was also present at their weekend meeting (Personal letter, Jan. 1, 1988).
- She recorded a solo collection on cassette tape, *Songs of My People*, noting that "songs of faith are my heritage."
- She videotaped conversations and interviews to help people cope with cancer and other serious illnesses.

The US Conference of Catholic Bishops experienced the depths of faith and human experience that Thea could deliver when she spoke at their gathering, in June 1989, in New Jersey. She was the first woman ever invited to address the Conference. Her speech "What Does It Mean to Be Black and Catholic?"

Cardboard cassette cover from the first release of
Songs of My People, with music from Thea as vocalist
and other musicians.

became legendary, inspiring the Bishops and all Catholics to "do the work" for economic justice, racial equality, and love for all people:

> What does it mean to be Black and Catholic? It means I come to my church fully function-ing . . . all that I am. . . .
>
> It means that the work of the ordained min-isters is to enable the people of God to go do the work of the Church. . . . The Church is calling us

to be participating and be involved. . . . Your job is to enable me . . . all of the people, to do the work of the Church in the world.

To be Black and Catholic means to get in touch with the world Church. . . . Within the Church, how do we work together so that we all have equal access? . . .

We have come a long way in faith. Just look at where we have come from . . . Many of you have walked and talked and prayed and worked with us. . . . I thank you.

Today, we are called to walk together in a new way toward that Land of Promise. And to celebrate who we are and whose we are. If we as church walk together—don't let nobody separate you, that's one thing Black folk can teach you, don't let folk divide you up. . . . The Church teaches us that the Church is a family, is a family of families, and the family got to stay together. . . .

If we walk and talk and work and play and stand together in Jesus's name, we'll be who we say we are: truly Catholic, and we shall overcome. Overcome the poverty. Overcome the loneliness. Overcome the alienation. And build together a holy city, a New Jerusalem, a city set apart, where they will know we are His because we love one another. ("Address to US Bishops," June 1989.)

After Thea's speech, she led the Bishops in slowly singing several verses of "We Shall Overcome," standing and swaying arm in arm, which brought some of them to tears.

Thea did all these things while fighting cancer. She continued to work to expand people's views and help people heal from whatever social harm, psychological hurts, or physical suffering had come their way. She reached out to all people, as Dr. Martin Luther King Jr. had done, unselfishly and without any profit in mind.

Sadly, in the midst of her outreach, Thea lost the last of her strength at age 52. She died and went home to God, in the words

Thea takes a break while traveling.
(Courtesy of Franciscan Sisters of Perpetual Adoration.)

of Sojourner Truth, "like a shooting star." At her peaceful moment of death on March 30, 1990, friend and travel companion Dorothy Kundinger, FSPA, was at her side.

In 2018, Servant of God Thea Bowman, FSPA, was voted by the US Conference of Catholic Bishops to advance in becoming named a saint for her faithful joy and ministering to others. Once she was named as a saint, Catholics would be able to pray for Thea's help with concerns or problems they encounter in their lives.

Thea's students, her friends, FSPA, and many people around the world continue her legacy by teaching and working in service to others in the fields of their choice, as their joyful and authentic selves. The spirituals continue to be sung, and her triumphs inspire young people to also triumph by setting high goals for themselves and by using their talents to joyfully serve other people.

TIMELINE OF THEA'S TRIUMPHS

1937 – Bertha (Birdie) Elizabeth Bowman is born to Dr. Theon and Mary Esther Bowman.

1947 – At age 9, Birdie tells her parents she wants to become a Catholic.

1949 – Birdie is enrolled in Grade 6, Holy Child Jesus School.

1952 – At age 15, Birdie tells her parents she wants to join the FSPA and study at St. Rose High School in La Crosse, Wisconsin, then go to college and become a teacher.

1953 – Birdie goes to La Crosse with Lina Putz, FSPA, on the train.

1953 – Birdie adjusts to a new culture and being far from home. She lives in a dorm and has a strict schedule. She is positive that she will do well in high school, and she does!

January 1955 – Birdie graduates from Saint Rose High School in La Crosse.

May 1955 to March 1956 – Birdie gets tuberculosis (TB) and misses her high school graduation ceremony in May. She recovers at River Pines Sanatorium in northern Wisconsin. She loses the whole first year of college, but triumphs by getting well and returning to Viterbo to start college.

1956 – On August 12, Birdie formally enters the FSPA and has a new name, Sister Mary Thea Bowman.

1958 – Sister Thea takes first vows to join the FSPA.

1959 – Sister Thea, age 21, begins teaching. She triumphs over school parents' prejudice by being professional and using her warm personality. She teaches students spirituals, and they enjoy exchanging letters and pictures with students at Holy Child Jesus.

1961 – Sister Thea returns to Canton to teach at Holy Child Jesus. She lives in the convent and enjoys Southern cooking and being near family. She leads a high school choir and records an album, adding her own poetry.

1961 to 1965 – Sister Thea spends summers at Viterbo College to finish a Bachelor of Arts degree.

1963 – Sister Thea takes her final, perpetual vows to join the FSPA.

1966 – The FSPA send Sister Thea to graduate school at Catholic American University in Washington, DC.

1969 – Sister Thea earns a Master of Arts degree in English.

1972 – Sister Thea earns a Doctor of Philosophy (PhD) in English and linguistics.

Fall 1972 to May 1978 – Sister Thea teaches at Viterbo College, becoming Chair of the English Department.

1974 – Sister Thea attends the Faulkner and Yoknapatawpha Conference, hosted by the University of Mississippi, where she becomes a popular presenter and speaker.

TIMELINE OF THEA'S TRIUMPHS

1974 to 1978 – Sister Thea takes student groups to Canton. Like "a bridge," she creates chances for students from different cultures to know and understand one another.

1978 – Sister Thea returns to Canton to take care of her elderly parents and to teach. She is appointed Director of Intercultural Awareness for the Catholic Diocese of Jackson and shortens her name to "Thea," still a member of the FSPA.

1979 and onward – Thea travels to preach faith, love, and spiritual healing by hosting revivals, lectures, and concerts.

1984 – Thea is diagnosed with cancer and begins treatments. Both parents die this same year. She continues to travel and host revivals, receiving many invitations.

1985 – Thea travels to Kenya and Tanzania to participate in a conference on racism. It is a triumph to visit Africa while undergoing cancer treatments.

1987 – Thea and friends appear on the TV news show *60 Minutes,* where she prompts interviewer Mike Wallace to say "Black is beautiful."

1989 – Thea speaks at the US Conference of Catholic Bishops and leads them in singing "We Shall Overcome." She is the first woman to address the Conference.

1990 – Thea dies peacefully on March 30.

2018 – Servant of God Thea Bowman, FSPA, is voted by the US Conference of Catholic Bishops to advance in becoming named a saint for her faithful joy and ministering to others.

GLOSSARY

aspirant The first step in becoming a member of the Franciscan Sisters of Adoration (FSPA); someone who hopes to achieve a goal, join a group, or accomplish something.

civil rights movement An ongoing, decades-long effort by Black people and supporters to gain the constitutional rights given to other groups in the United States, such as voting and property ownership rights.

convent A house or building where Catholic nuns lived as a community.

elder A person who is older than middle age and known to be wise.

first vows A woman takes first vows of poverty, chastity, and obedience to show she wants to live according to these values and commit to joining the Franciscan Sisters of Adoration (FSPA). She chooses a new name of personal meaning to go along with her new choice and way of life.

Great Depression A period of world history, 1929 to 1939, when many people were extremely poor and jobs were hard to find. Farmers in the United States lost their farms due to a long drought called the Dust Bowl. People in cities and in the countryside needed help from the government to get food, clothing, and shelter.

irrational   Thinking or feeling without logic or reason.

juke joint   A place where local people ate, drank, danced, and listened to live music in the twentieth century.

Maasai   An ethnic group that lives in northern, central, and southern Kenya and northern Tanzania.

perpetual vows   For women who have studied and prepared to join the FSPA, these vows are a lifelong promise to live according to the FSPA principles of poverty, chastity, and obedience.

postulant   The final stage of studying and preparing before a woman joins the FSPA.

potluck   A unplanned dinner where people gather and bring food to share.

prejudice   Biased or negative feelings or actions against someone or something, without a firm reason.

raucous   Rowdy or loud.

Roman Catholic Church   A religion that includes faith in the Old Testament and New Testament of the Bible; its organization is led by the Pope, who lives in Rome.

segregation   A series of laws in some states that barred Black people from rights and privileges given to white people. The laws were eventually proven to be unfair and unconstitutional.

self-determination   A person's vision, focus, and efforts to become who they want to become as an adult, which guides the person's decisions and actions.

Sojourner Truth (1797–1883)   An abolitionist and women's
rights advocate. While enslaved, she fought for and won
the right to be free with her children.

spirituals   Songs sung with a spiritual reason and in a
religious tradition, whether to express emotions or the
singer's faith, to pray, to lament, or to celebrate.

tuberculosis (TB)   A deadly disease for which a drug first
became available in 1949. Some sanitoriums to isolate and
cure patients with TB started closing during the 1950s.

voting rights   The right for a citizen who is age 18 and
older to vote in each local, state, and federal election in the
United States and its territories.

SOURCES

"Are You Walkin' with Me? Sister Thea Bowman, William Faulkner, and African-American Culture." Video produced by Lisa Neumann Howorth. Center for the Study of Southern Culture, University of Mississippi. July 1990. Used with permission. Retrieved and transcribed by the author from vimeo.com/11113853.

Bowman, Thea, "Address to US Bishops." June 1989. Speech at the United States Conference of Catholic Bishops, June 1989. Retrieved and transcribed by the author from https://www.youtube.com/watch?v=uOV0nQkjuoA.

Bowman, Thea. Personal letter to the author from Canton, MS. December 26, 1985.

Bowman, Thea. Personal letter to the author from Canton, MS. 1987 (undated).

Bowman, Thea. Personal letter to the author from Canton, MS. January 1, 1988.

Gschwind, S. Mary Ann, FSPA. Interview by the author. La Crosse, WI. March 18, 2019.

Holy Child Singers, vocalists. *The Voice of Negro America*. Directed by Sister M. Thea Bowman. Produced by Holy Child Jesus School, a Trinity Mission School, Canton, MS. Recorded in 1965, LP record. Poetry excerpt transcribed by the author.

Potaracke, S. Rochelle, FSPA. Interview by the author. La Crosse, WI. March 18, 2019.

Schutz, Aaron. "Misunderstanding Mississippi, 1964: The Freedom Schools and the Embrace of Personalist Pedagogy." Unpublished chapter for *Social Class, Social Action, and Education*. New York: Palgrave Macmillan, 2010. Used with permission.

Smith, Charlene, and John Feister. *Thea's Song: The Life of Thea Bowman*. Maryknoll, NY: Orbis Books, 2009. Used with permission.

Student participant in Viterbo College trip to Canton. Interview by the author. March 2020.

Thea Bowman: In My Own Words. Edited by Maurice J. Nutt. Ligouri, MO: Ligouri Publications, 2009, pages 3, 4, 6, 64, 90. Used with permission.

IMAGE CREDITS

Bowman, Thea. *Sister Thea: Songs of My People.* Released by Krystal Records in 1988, cassette cover (cardboard). Original provided by the author.

Courtesy of Franciscan Sisters of Perpetual Adoration (FSPA) at fspa.org/theabowman. Used with permission.

Imprints, Volume 2. Student yearbook. Viterbo College, La Crosse, WI, 1971, page 41 (Thea returns to Viterbo to teach). Photographer unknown. Used with permission of Viterbo University.

Imprints, Volume 3. Student yearbook. Viterbo College, La Crosse, WI, 1972, page 43 (Hallelujah Singers). Photographer unknown. Used with permission of Viterbo University.

Imprints, Volume 6. Student yearbook. Viterbo College, La Crosse, WI, 1975, page 42 (Thea laughing in classroom). Photographer unknown. Used with permission of Viterbo University.

Imprints, Volume 8. Student yearbook. Viterbo College, La Crosse, WI, 1977, page 120 (Lunchtime in Canton). Photographer unknown. Used with permission of Viterbo University.

Sojourner, Sue (Lorenzi) (1941–2020). "The Older Mileston Women in the Holmes Co., Mississippi Community Center at Mileston, 1965." Photograph print. Used with permission of Aaron Sojourner.

FURTHER READING

Catholic Diocese of Jackson. "Biography." *Sister Thea Bowman Cause for Canonization.* Retrieved from http://sistertheabowman.com/biography/

Donohue, S. Celeste. "A Prayer: S. Thea Bowman, FSPA." Pamphlet. Anderson, SC: The Franciscans. Retrieved from https://www.fspa.org/uploads/content_files/files/Theaprayercard_000%281%29.pdf

Sojourner, Sue Lorenzi, with Cheryl Reitan. *Thunder of Freedom: Black Leadership and the Transformation of 1960s Mississippi.* Lexington, KY: University Press of Kentucky, 2013.

Thea Bowman: Handing on Her Legacy. Edited by C. Koontz. Kansas City, MO: Sheed & Ward, 1991.

ABOUT THE AUTHOR

MARY G. VERRILL is a writer and musician. She earned the degree of Bachelor of Arts in English at Viterbo University with Dr. Thea Bowman, FSPA, as her professor and thesis mentor, along with a Minor in Music in 1978. Some memories of literature classes with Thea are included in this book. Due to the excellent preparation for graduate school she received from Thea and other faculty, she completed the degree of Master of Arts in English Literature at the University of Wisconsin–Madison in 1980. Wanting to spread the joy of teaching and learning witnessed while a student of Thea, Verrill taught college writing and literature courses as adjunct faculty in Minnesota and Wisconsin. She earned the degree of Doctor of Education (EdD) in Leadership at Saint Mary's University of Minnesota in 2015. She continues to write, teach, and play violin.